T0113686

GO AHEAD

Daily Devotional

WILLIAM M. SHELTON

authorHOUSE®

AuthorHouse™
1663 Liberty Drive
Bloomington, IN 47403
www.authorhouse.com
Phone: 833-262-8899

Published by AuthorHouse 08/09/2022

ISBN: 978-1-6655-6762-6 (sc)
ISBN: 978-1-6655-6761-9 (e)

Library of Congress Control Number: 2022914502

Print information available on the last page.

This book is printed on acid-free paper.

CONTENTS

MEN'S DEVOTIONAL

Uplifting and inspiring devotionals for the man/husband/father who wants a real relationship with Jesus Christ and lives according to the Kingdom of God's principles.

Every other Wednesday, a devotional based on a scriptural focus or theme is shared with men, mostly African Americans, from every walk of life but with a common need: a personal and saving relationship with Christ. To know God is to know His Word, and we submit ourselves to the authority of God's Word in a society where morals, absolutes, ideals, and convictions are subject to the whims of man instead of Scripture.

Each devotional is concluded with the words "GO. AHEAD!" since we believe inspiration translates into action which shows both faith and application in our daily lives.

Your humble servant,
William M. Shelton

A BOOK OF REMEMBRANCE

Then those who feared the LORD spoke with one another. The Lord paid attention and heard them, and a book of remembrance was written before him of those who feared the LORD and esteemed his name. **-Malachi 3:16 AMP**

First, I'm humbled that you would allow me to share God's word with you twice a month (over 40 men now).

Secondly, I want to say thank you for the many ways, times, and opportunities some of you have shared God's Word with me through individual texts, on the men's group chats, or when we talk on the phone. Amid so much chaos and uncertainty in our land, God's Word has been our truth, our stability, and our strength... which reminds me of this precious verse in Malachi.

When two people who reverence the LORD speak to one another about His goodness, protection, faithfulness, righteousness, mercy, grace, love, and salvation, a book is being recorded of our conversations. There is no greater or more urgent topic than the One who can save us and deliver us from all sin: Jesus Christ, our Savior and Lord.

So please continue to talk about the Lord God, the Most High, with each other as often as you can. He listens and he hears us when we do.

GO. AHEAD!

A CALL TO SERVANTHOOD/ GREATNESS

1 Samuel 16:17-18 NET

So Saul said to his attendants, "Find someone who plays well and bring him to me." One of the servants answered, "I have seen a son of Jesse of Bethlehem who knows how to play the lyre. He is a brave man and a warrior. He speaks well and is a fine-looking man. And the Lord is with him."

Imagine that in a particular area of your life you were called "up" to a higher position or appointment. What about the job where you work? What would you do if they made you a supervisor or manager right now? What if your salary was tripled right immediately for doing the same work? What if you had access to all inside and sensitive information about a company or an organization where you work? What if, suddenly, you were trusted with someone else's house, car, money, and personal possessions?

COULD YOU HANDLE IT? ARE YOU TRULY READY FOR THE CALL "UP"?

David, a shepherd boy, went to bring lunch to his older brothers serving in the army of Israel and heard this giant Philistine soldier taunting the men and defying their God. He successfully kills the giant Goliath with a slingshot and a stone. How was he able to do it? Through his training in the field with the sheep. He had experience with bears and lions trying to harm his father's sheep, and he knew how to deal with them. Later, God allowed an evil spirit to torture King Saul for his disobedience; Saul asked for a man who could play an instrument skillfully and provide him some relief. Someone in his court remembered David and they called for him—the king's court "called" for David—so he went "up" to the palace.

Brethren, please look at David's resume:

- a skillful musician
- a brave young man
- a proven warrior
- wise and well-spoken, handsome
- The Lord's anointing is on his life

Do you see the list of attributes spoken by the king's servant about this young man, David? Look at the last statement of the servant— "The LORD is with him!"

If you and I are ever called "up" to greatness, we need to remember that we are first being called to serve. Greatness comes through the right preparation and the right heart/attitude. You can be called "up" but then come crashing "down" if you don't possess the qualities of a godly man submitted unto the Lord's will.

David accepted the call to the king's court and became Saul's armor-bearer as well as his musician.

Some years later (around 12), he became King of Israel. He served first and then he became great…

GO. AHEAD! Serve and become great.

A GOOD CONFESSION

12. Fight the good fight of the faith. Take hold of the eternal life to which you were called when you made your good confession in the presence of many witnesses. 13. In the sight of God, who gives life to everything, and of Christ Jesus, who while testifying before Pontius Pilate made the good confession. **(1 Timothy 6:12-13) NIV**

Proclaiming your love and submission to Jesus Christ around other believers is easy and it should be. You are with people who have made the same decision and the same commitment to follow Christ, no matter the cost. *But even though it's easy, it's also necessary. It is meant to build you up in your faith* (Jude 1:20 NIV).

You and I make a good confession around other witnesses, because one day you and I will be required to make that same and equally powerful confession to someone who is against us—does not believe or subscribe to our beliefs or convictions—who may even hate our Lord and Savior!

What will you do when that day comes? Shy away and remain silent, or will you be bold in the Holy Spirit and declare that Jesus is Lord of your life and that you trust in him? Some of us have a wrong understanding about worshipping with other believers—it does bring clarity to our proclamation; it does bring strength to our witness; and it does bring a conviction to speak for Him to those who would deny Him. I don't see how anyone could do this being alone all the time.

Jesus says He sings in the midst of His brethren, and the scriptures tell us not to abandon ourselves, as some do, but to encourage and motivate one another (Heb. 2:12, Heb. 10:25 NIV).

Our confession to God today in the presence of each other will embolden us tomorrow to have that same profession in the presence of our enemies. Jesus told Pilate that His kingdom was not of this world—that it was a kingdom of truth and all who knew the truth would hear Him.

What a testimony! You're next.

GO. AHEAD!

A MAN WHO TREMBLES

...but to this man will I look, even to him that is poor and of a contrite spirit, and trembleth (has great reverence) at my word. **(Isaiah 66:2) KJV**

I equate being a man with having strength. I believe that is part of our DNA makeup as men; considering ourselves as bearers of strength, we welcome the challenge, so to speak, the "weight" of the situation, posturing a fearless attitude even in the face of danger. However, there is a time for great reverence; the Hebrew word tremble (charad) even suggests fear-and it concerns the Word of God.

So, let me pause here and ask a question... do you revere God's Word? Are you truly aware of who the Everlasting GOD, the LORD, the Creator of the ends of the earth is?

He asserts His authority in the first verse by stating his station of rest and then boldly reminds us in verse 2 that He is the One who made the heavens and the earth—no one else was around. He did it all by himself.

However, in the midst of God's awesome and amazing power, He will take the time to look down on the earth and pay particular attention to a man who trembles at the Word.

A man who hears God's Word and knows he has "missed the mark" (sin) and needs to be changed from the inside out; a man who reads God's Word and asks for the power of the Holy Spirit to work on his mind, thoughts, behavior, and actions; *a man who receives the Word with joy because he truly understands the alternative of rejecting the Word and the One who gives it* (Heb. 10:31 NIV).

God will pay close attention to the man/father/husband who truly respects His Word and is willing and ready to make a change.

Guess what... He'll send help.

GO. AHEAD!

ADAM'S EMPLOYMENT

And the Lord God took the man, and put him into the Garden of Eden to dress it and to keep it. **-Genesis 2:15 KJV**

When you think about Adam, the first man created, which picture or illustration stands out more in your mind? 1) the one with him working in the garden, dressing it and keeping it, or 2) him wrapped in fig leaves, hiding from God?

After the Everlasting God creates the earth and everything in it and rests, he then places the first man, Adam, in the garden and employs him to bless him. Yes, yes, you heard that right! There is nothing about Adam's employment (enabled by God) that's drenched in exertion, worry, frustration, fatigue, or sorrow. Adam takes his God-given intellect, authority, and creativity and does what God created him to do: govern and rule over God's creation.

Genesis 2:15-24 KJV teaches us that work is a blessing from God. God puts Adam to work because he wants Adam to discover some things about himself and his Creator.

1. Dress and keep the garden.
2. Names ALL of the animals and created beings God brings to him.
3. In Adam's work, God allows him to discover an inward desire for a more intimate relationship.
4. God blesses Adam again! (brings his wife to him).

Work helps you and I discover things about our Heavenly Father and ourselves. That is why we work as unto the Lord and not man —Colossians 3:23 KJV. As men, we are called to produce, create, manage, and rest, all the while glorifying God and worshipping Him in our endeavors.

Brother, get up off that couch-God has something He wants you to do!

We **Work** and we **Discover.**

GO. AHEAD!

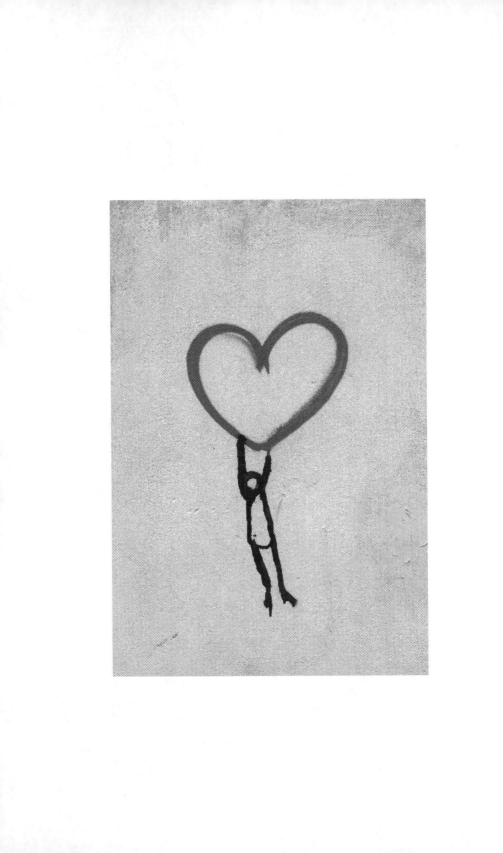

ALWAYS PRAY. DON'T LOSE HEART

One day Jesus told his disciples a story to show that they should always pray and never give up. The passage is in Luke 18:1 (NLT).

Confession: **I don't pray enough**.

I'm a pastor and I'm always in service or meetings where prayer is part of the agenda, but I still don't pray enough.

I lead prayer services during the week, and I pray for people who are facing crises or sick in the hospital, but I still don't pray enough.

If I prayed more, justice would be served in the lives of many I'm concerned about. Deliverance, breakthrough, healing, and victory would be a reality in the lives of people I care about. My children would benefit from me praying more. I know my wife would… our parents and family members on both sides would be blessed, even saved, if only I prayed more.

You see, every man who is reading this should be praying and not giving up. There is so much happening in our world today that it can cause us to retreat into a corner and stop praying. We begin to substitute fervent prayer with wishful thinking… or we abandon the place of prayer for a place of comfort. If only MEN prayed more!

We should always be praying and never faint or lose heart. A widow, with no husband and no family, requests justice from a judge who doesn't fear God nor respect people. He keeps dismissing her and her case; he has no time to be bothered with her. Yet this widow keeps coming to him, asking for justice. This judge, who cares nothing about God or people, finally gives her the justice she seeks!

How much more will God grant justice to His children who cry out to Him day and night? But brethren, we are not crying out to God. Our families, communities, churches, and nation are getting worse, and we won't approach God with tears. You and I can't wear him out; he's inexhaustible. And, unlike the unjust judge, the God of Heaven and Earth loves humanity; Jesus Christ died for humanity because He is LOVE.

In addition, I don't believe praying "more" just means praying longer. We should be praying with intention, purpose, and with conviction. Pray when our hearts are moved, and by all means, pray when the Holy Spirit directs us to pray. Some years ago, people would say, "Keep me in your prayers," and I would say, "sure"—only to forget and then remember in a panic a week later. Now I pray for them right then and there. I take them and their concern to Jesus, the Righteous Judge, and pray until something happens. Prayer: Father God, I need to pray more.

I can't lose heart. I'll pray instead.

GO. AHEAD!

BE THE CHANGE

Mahatma Gandhi is credited with the saying, "Become the change you want to see in the world".

Well, recent tragedies and polarizing topics (abortion, gender, race) definitely speak to the need for change in our nation and world. If change is needed, and it is, how will you and I become that change? Will we donate time, serve our community, share knowledge and resources, develop relationships with those who need it most, and speak the truth in love?

Exactly how will we become that change? Before we attempt to answer that question, let's deal with this one first: have WE CHANGED?

Have we allowed and submitted ourselves to the internal workings that bring about real change? If we're doing the same thing we were doing five years ago, I doubt we're changing, we're simply existing and getting by. Real change is difficult and it requires pain, challenge, honesty, and truth. So, brothers, do we truly desire to become the change we want to see in the world?

2 Corinthians 5:17 NET says, *"So then, if anyone is in Christ, he is a new creation; what is old has passed away – look, what is new has come!*

If you're in Christ, you have been changed, transformed even as the Greek meaning suggests. Then, by conclusion, those in Christ have been changed by the power of God and have been given the assignment to go and bring change in the world.

So back to our first question: where do we start? It's overwhelming to think about if we're truly honest. May I suggest that you "**be**"?

BE what Christ has called you to be in this world: salt and light.

Don't lose your ability to influence (season) others and don't take your influence "light" and hide it under a bed or barrel.

Just "be" in Christ. I'm starting now. Brothers feel free to join me.

GO. AHEAD!

BETTER IS THE END
OF A THING...

How does the first month of a new year treat you? Or rather, how do YOU treat the first month of a brand-new year?

Expecting things to go great or better than expected? Good for you.

Are you more of a pragmatist, just taking things as they come? Do you have any expectations that things will change? It's an entire year, mind you, and a lot can happen in a year's time.

Hopefully, I pray no one is going through a more difficult time than last year. But if so, the grace and mercy of God will manifest in your life like never before. All of us are on different parts of our journey, and each part of the journey is important for our growth and character-building. Some got off to a great start this year, while others are still searching, questioning, and seeking.

The Preacher in Ecclesiastes 7:8 NET gives us some perspective:

Better is the end of a thing than the beginning thereof: and the patient in spirit is better than the proud in spirit.

It's important to understand that adversity now does not mean adversity later. And conversely, success today does not always prevent a challenge tomorrow. The "end" of something means it has been established, made firm, or stable. Let us be reminded that "we" (men, brethren) want to be made better—not just our incomes, residences, or automobiles—our spirits and our faith in God need to be established. Oh yes, the end of a thing is certainly better than its beginning.

The Preacher also reminds us that patience is better than pride. Trust and obedience to Christ Jesus are indicators of patience. Pride says, "I don't need God, nor do I need people." Please, brothers, don't have that mindset.

Every new year and each new day, **you and I** are going to get better! GO. AHEAD!

BORN FOR ADVERSITY...

A friend loves at all times, and a brother is born for adversity.
Proverbs 17:17 NIV

Jesus, the greatest teacher in the world, had only a few disciples who followed him everywhere he went. Yes, Jesus had other disciples and followers, but this committed group of men was hand-picked by him. And when things got tough, he confided in and relied on three of them (Peter, James, and John).

We live in a world where everyone is obsessed with online followers, subscribers, likes, and retweets. Our "friends" on social media networks are nothing more than mere acquaintances. We don't know them, nor do they know us.

If real trouble or a crisis was to hit your life, only one or two people would be there to help lift you up. Knowing this, I want to encourage us to be "a friend" or "a brother" as shown in this verse.

What exactly does that mean? It means having real relationships that endure, sustain, and even grow in times of adversity. Unfortunate circumstances and difficult times are becoming more real in our communities, and what is needed now are men who are not afraid to stand and show up when adversity comes. Be a "man" and love not just when it's convenient but love at all times; be courageous enough to roll up your sleeves and help ease another man's burden.

Society is training us to be popular, while God wants us to be present.

Be a true friend to someone… Be a real brother to somebody… born for difficult times.

GO. AHEAD!

CONFLICT ...AGAIN?

I try not to... I really do... but I'm learning that offenses are unavoidable. What is always in my power is how I respond to them. As a disciple of Christ, I'm obligated to respond appropriately. Consider the words spoken in Luke 17:1 (NET)

Jesus said to his disciples, "Stumbling blocks (offenses) are sure to come, but woe to the one through whom they come!

Jesus' words prick our conscience and command our attention: you can't avoid offenses, but WOE to the person through whom it comes. Simply put, you and I cannot be the initiators, creators, manufacturers, and designers of any human conflict/offense/disagreement and then deny God's power to reconcile us to Him and restore our relationship with that person or individual.

On one of the world's biggest stages this past Sunday night (the Oscars), we witnessed an "offense" and a "response". (I'll let each of you decide who spoke and acted in the wrong or right that evening).

... you see, I'm reminded neither of those persons professes to be disciples of Jesus Christ. **Hopefully, you all are**. Let's show each other and the world that resolution to all human conflict is inside of you (it's Christ, the perfect mediator).

GO. AHEAD!

BLESSING
CURSE

THE CONTRADICTION
OF THE TONGUE

With the tongue we bless our Lord and Father, and with it we curse people who are made in God's likeness. Blessing and cursing come out of the same mouth. My brothers and sisters, these things should not be this way. -James 3: 9-10 CSB

This unruly tongue of ours, described as evil and poisonous, shows its ugliness in how we talk and speak of one another. In one breath, we use our tongues to bless God, and in the next breath, we use that same mouth to curse men. Let us be reminded that the men we curse, slander, and gossip about are made in the image of God. And yet, we refuse to recognize this truth, ignoring the implications of our words, and we speak evil towards and against our brother.

And if verse 9 does not bring us to shame, certainly the next verse should: **My brothers and sisters, these things should not be!** Those who have been born again of the Spirit, partakers of the divine nature and forgiven of their sins, are to rely upon the power of the Holy Spirit for our tongues to be controlled. There can be NO contradiction between our words and our faith. *The world is sick and tired of hypocrites who "say" one thing and "do" another, but those in the community of faith - the Lord's Church are held to the highest standard and constantly reminded to love one another* (John 15:12,17 NIV).

Dr. Matthew Henry said that completely opposite effects from the same causes are monstrous and not to be found in nature... wow!

A fountain bringing sweet AND bitter water? **C'mon now...**

A fig tree bearing olives or a vine bearing figs? **What's up with that?**

Why would anyone travel to the lowest body of water on earth, the Dead Sea, and demand that it bring forth fresh spring water and life? **It can't by its own nature!**

If we curse men with our tongues, it's against the very nature of God - and if cursing comes out the same mouth as blessings, then we need to find out what's really going on inside. Your mouth gives away what's going on in your heart. The Holy Spirit can help us.

GO. AHEAD!

GET HOME SAFE

Everyone must submit to governing authorities. For all authority comes from God, and those in positions of authority have been placed there by God. -**Romans 13:1 NLT**

So you must submit to them, not only to avoid punishment, but also to keep a clear conscience. -**Romans 13:5 NLT**

When I'm driving and I see a police car or hear its siren, I don't get nervous because I know I haven't broken any laws. The law is not for the law-abiding citizen, but for the lawbreaker. So, I go on about my business as usual. However, if I see the police car riding directly behind me and flashing its lights for me to pull over, I'm obligated to. It doesn't matter if I "like" the police or not… I find a safe place and pull over because of the authority of the officer.

You see, I understand that the officer doesn't have any authority by himself; it was given to him by an authority agency much higher than him. This is pretty much what Jesus told Pilate: *"you would have no power over me at all except it were given you from above"* (John 19:11 NLT).

That power that Jesus was talking about was from God, His Father. You and I pull over because we understand the authority the officer has comes from the One we serve and worship: Christ Jesus the LORD (He has ALL authority in heaven and earth).

The key/goal/aim after getting pulled over is to **get home safely!**

Get home to your wife so you can make love to her; get home to your kids so you can spend time with them; get back home safe so you can eat dinner and maybe watch the game afterward; get home safe so you can get some sleep and get up in the morning to go to work. But **none** of that will happen if you and I disobey and rebel against the authority that is requesting us to do something.

If you and I resist, there is a consequence. That "consequence" used to be a resisting arrest charge or having a fine levied against us-now it is death my friend... a life ended tragically because it wouldn't submit. You're not just submitting to a police officer, but you are ultimately submitting to GOD himself!

Eccl 10:4 teaches us that if the spirit of the ruler rises up against you, leave not your place; for yielding pacifies great offenses. Resisting will always make matters worse—we see the tragic results almost every week on the news and social media.

Brethren, we're not weak if we submit-we show how strong we are in Christ. He submitted his life unto a greater good: to die for the sins of unrighteous and rebellious men so they could be called "sons of God"!

GO. AHEAD!

HE DOES ALL THINGS WELL

Jesus got up and went away from there to the region of Tyre. And when He had entered a house, He wanted no one to know of it; yet He could not escape notice.

Again He went out from the region of Tyre, and came through Sidon to the Sea of Galilee, within the region of Decapolis.

They were utterly astonished, saying, *"He has done all things well; He makes even the deaf to hear and the mute to speak."* **(Mark 7: 24, 31, 37 NASB)**

One day, Jesus gets up and goes into the borders of Tyre and Sidon. He doesn't want anyone to notice. He then leaves the coasts of Tyre and Sidon and travels through the coasts of Decapolis. Some interesting things happened on these two trips.

First, a woman begs Jesus to heal her daughter of an unclean spirit. And later, the people of the village beg Jesus to touch a man who is deaf and has difficulty speaking. We find Jesus going about his daily schedule, touching people, impacting their lives, and changing them forever; a desperate woman tired of seeing her daughter afflicted by the devil; and a desperate community who wants to see a man set free from a deaf and mute spirit.

Jesus responds with immediacy and compassion. And His work is complete; nothing left to chance; no need for a repeat visit or follow-up; he touches people and they are healed completely. <u>Jesus does all things well!</u> **Everything He does is good**.

We often try to do "well" and, in the process, we sometimes fail miserably. We realize our limitations, shortcomings, and weaknesses in our pursuit of good. It's in these moments when we agree, like the community did, that Jesus and only him have done all things well. He makes the spiritually deaf to hear God's glorious Word and the spiritually mute to speak and sing of His wondrous power.

The Scriptures declare in Col. 1:27 KJV - *Christ in you, the hope of glory.*

That is the only way you and I can do things well as He did.

GO. AHEAD!

HOPE DELAYED

Hope deferred makes the heart sick, but when the desire comes, it is a tree of life. -**Proverbs 13:12 MEV**

David Guzik wrote that **the strength of hope sustains the heart.** So, brothers, what are you hoping for right now? What expectations do you have for yourself or for the people you love and care about? Any goals, dreams, or plans lately?

All men hope, desire, and long for something; the Bible makes this clear. But it must come with correction and discipline: being able to <u>receive instruction</u> and being **willing** to be diligent in hard work.

Verse 4 of the same chapter says:

The slacker craves, yet has nothing, but the diligent is fully satisfied. (CSB)

Brothers, I can't help but wonder what this looks like in the spiritual realm. Those who are diligent in seeking the Lord and have a desire to be more like Jesus (especially in a time like now) will be satisfied!

There are times when our hope feels like it's being delayed and drawn out **(e.g., need a better paying job, desire a stronger marriage, want to get in better shape)**—this is the moment where we stop and remind ourselves that the fulfillment will bring sustained life like a tree planted in our back yard. And so, we keep our eyes on God, our true hope and expectation.

He is never late and always on time!

GO. AHEAD!

IRON SHARPENS IRON...

One of the least respected words in the body of Christ, especially among men, is "accountability."

We have somehow deceived ourselves into thinking we are answerable to no one; we are free to do what we want without any questions or concerns.

And yet, accountability seems to be an important part of discipleship and Christian growth because when the church attempts to have any type of men's ministry or men's fellowship, we pull out this verse:

Iron sharpeneth iron; so a man sharpeneth the countenance of his friend. Proverbs 27:17 KJV

This one verse <u>demands</u> accountability among men. If you take two large knives and place them in separate cabinet drawers, how would they be able to sharpen each other? You see, every new knife is sharp straight out of the box, but over time and continued use, it begins to dull and lose its effectiveness. It needs another knife to be resharpened. Notice that only iron can sharpen iron.... wood and paper cannot. May I translate it a little further? Only iron is able to hammer out and smooth the rough spots in another piece of iron. Only the "wounds" of a friend/Christian brother/ another man can help deal with certain areas in our lives that are suspect. (Prov. 27:6 NIV)

Every man (who confesses he is saved) must be willing to allow a born-again, spirit-filled man to deal with him; this is not easy but necessary so we can be sharpened. We, as men, do not like to be confronted or challenged—and yet scripture shows us there are times when another man or brother must do so.

Are you willing my brethren? I am. I have to.

GO, AHEAD!

LAST ADAM

"For as by one man's disobedience many were made sinners, so by the obedience of one shall many be made righteous." -Romans 5:19 KJV

The first Adam affected the entire human race with a willful act of disobedience. The "last Adam," Jesus Christ, affected all of mankind with an act of total submission to His Father's will.

I want to be like the last Adam—don't you?

We can... and it starts with obedience to God... dying to our old nature, being born again with a new spirit.

Brothers, we died under the first Adam but are made alive by Christ! GO. AHEAD!

LEADERSHIP

G ood morning, brothers. I'll keep my words brief today.
Every man on this group chat is a leader. You absolutely are.

LEADERSHIP = Influence

Influence is the capacity to affect the character, development, or behavior of someone else.

Right now, during this crisis in our nation, "how" are you leading?
Go make a difference out there. Lead the right way!
GO. AHEAD!

LIFEBLOOD

Noun: The blood considered essential to maintain life.

In the past two weeks, there has been more bloodshed from mass shooters in public spaces and schools; gang violence in major cities; and domestic disputes in both urban and rural communities than I can keep track of. To be honest, brethren, I am emotionally fatigued and troubled at the condition of the human heart in America.

Then the Holy Spirit reminded me of God's Word: ***Sin will be rampant everywhere, and the love of many will grow cold.*** (Matthew 24:12 NLT)

I'll leave the discussion to others who are more qualified to decide whether we have a gun control issue and, if so, what should be done. What I'm certain of is that we have a sin issue, and it's growing in frequency and intensity.

In Genesis 9, after the floodwaters recede, God instructs and reminds Noah of the command to multiply and replenish the earth. He allows man to eat meat for the first time (*...every moving thing shall be meat for you...v. 3*) but forbids him to eat meat with its blood in it; for the life is in the blood.

And then the command is expanded in verse **6: Whoever sheds human blood, by humans shall his blood be shed.**

That's pretty straightforward. But then the reason for this command is given:... **for in the image of God made him man.**

<u>Every man is created in the image of God</u>; not a beast, bird, insect, or some abstract object, but in God's likeness and resemblance. The Almighty God, Yahweh, thought it important enough to make humanity in His image and partakers of His divine nature. For any human to carelessly/thoughtlessly take the life of another human is a violation against God the Creator and His will and purpose for all human life.

Why am I sharing this with you today? Because the shed blood of those innocent and righteous has the ability to "testify" to God. He told Cain that his brother's blood (Abel) cries out to him from the ground. *When Jesus' blood was shed it "spoke" better things than that of Abel* (Heb. 12:24 NLT).

Brothers, I truly believe the innocent blood of little children, elderly citizens, and targeted individuals based on race or religion are crying out to God, and retribution will be meted out to this nation-we must repent and repent soon. America has a moral obligation to restrain sin, or there will be a reckoning. Please pray for hurting families today.

GO. AHEAD!

NOTE: THIS DEVOTIONAL FOCUS IS NOT AN INDICTMENT/ CHARGE AGAINST THOSE WHO WORK IN LAW ENFORCEMENT OR WHERE HUMAN LIFE IS THREATENED AND PROTECTION MUST BE/ IS USED.

LOOKING OUT MY WINDOW

"At the window of my house, I looked through my lattice." -**Proverbs 7:6 NIV**

Here is what we can gather about the storyteller in chapter 7:

The storyteller is a father. He has a son he's concerned about.

Over time, the storyteller has seen many young men make unwise decisions.

He feels it's his duty to warn his son and others about the grave danger awaiting them.

The storyteller provides a much better option for one's preservation and safety.

The storyteller is obviously Solomon the king. He is teaching his son about sex education and warns him of sexual immorality personified as a strange woman, a woman on the prowl and on the loose, hunting for victims.

Let me pause and share this quickly: The Book of Proverbs is a collection of wise sayings developed over time and derived from practical experience.

Solomon is telling his son that every day when he looks out his window, he sees young man after young man make an unwise decision: they cross the street near "her" corner and stroll down the road to "her" house. He looks out his window every night and sees the same result—even strong men suffer the same fate as the young and inexperienced. Many don't make it out alive.

Solomon the storyteller warns his son, just as our Father in Heaven is warning us as sons, to stay away from sexual sin at all costs... It could cost you your life!

But wait, there is another woman in the streets, and she is calling out to the men, and her name is Wisdom (chapter 8). She represents God's perspective on every matter of life. Choose this woman instead, my brother; she (Wisdom) may very well save your life!

GO. AHEAD!

MURMURINGS

And Moses and Aaron said to all the Israelites, "In the evening you will know that the LORD has brought you out of the land of Egypt, and in the morning, you shall see the glory of the LORD, because He has heard your murmurings against the LORD. As for us, what are we, that you should murmur against us?" -Exodus 16:6-7 NASB

The precious believers in Philippi went through much suffering and persecution for their faith in Christ Jesus. In addition, they experienced conflict amongst each other, which is why the words "fellowship" "love" and "joy" are major themes in Philippians.

Hardship and suffering have unique effects on the human heart and its response. In our hurt and pain, we lash out at people to attach blame to alleviate what we are experiencing. There are moments in our lives when, if we're honest, we are upset at God.

The Israelites, one month removed from Egypt and in the Wilderness of Sin, complain against Moses and Aaron because there's not enough food. Supplies are scarce; they've used almost everything, and now they murmur against the leaders, Moses and Aaron.

This is basically what they said: "You had God lead us out here in the desert to starve to death—we could have stayed in Egypt and done that!"

So, there you have it... GOD is the real issue. Their complaint, at its core, is their inability to trust the LORD in their greatest time of need.

The Philippian church, in all its conflict and opposition, is instructed in Philippians 2:14 MOUNCE *"Do all things without grumbling or arguing"*.

Don't ever murmur against the providence of God or another believer.

It's a trap Satan uses to keep you and me from trusting the Most High God and glorifying Him with other believers. Instead of complaining, let praise be our attitude.

GO. AHEAD!

NOT IN CONTROL

1 Chronicles 16:31 (NET Bible)

Let the heavens rejoice, and the earth be happy! Let the nations say, "The Lord reigns!"

This past week, I was humbly reminded of something I already knew: I am NOT in control. I tend to forget that from time to time, so last week, God patiently and lovingly reminded me that He is sovereign, is in complete control and simply wants me to trust Him.

I like to get things done… I like to check things off my list. But Father-God moved at His own pace in my life and wanted me to pause and be in awe of Him.

I heard a pastor on TV say that we need to be released from the allusion that we are in control. I agree with him-we are not in control, never have been and never will be. When things (both good and bad) come into our lives, we are to "manage" them with prayer, trust, wisdom, discernment, and hope. We are to put our entire weight on Christ Jesus because he loves us (1 Peter 5:7 NET); this is the intended meaning in the Greek language.

Brethren, you and I do not have the power or privilege to do whatever we want when we want—that is reserved only for God (Psalms 115:3 NET). We are to seek Him each day for our "daily bread" and know there is enough grace to handle what comes our way.

Trust Him for TODAY-leave TOMORROW in His hands.

GOD's in CONTROL (He's got it!)

GO. AHEAD!

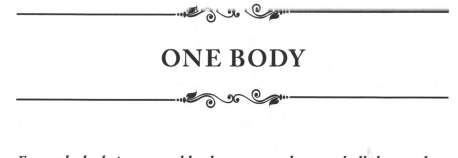

ONE BODY

For as the body is one, and hath many members, and all the members of that one body, being many, are one body: so also is Christ. 1 Corinthians 12:12 KJV

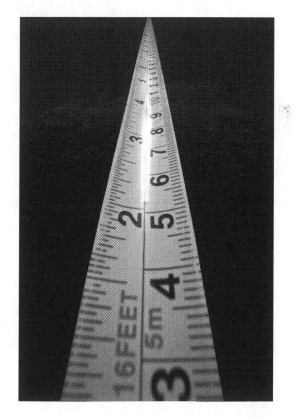

D o me a favor: you and another man or brother grab a tape measure. You hold the hook part and let him walk away from you holding the case. Tell him to stop whenever he feels like it. Now YOU guess the distance? You can't! The other brother has the measurement on his end. He knows the exact distance. Yea, you could guess—you might even get close, but you would be off by more than a few inches—and that could be the difference between success and failure in what you're trying to build. This country celebrates Independence Day on July 4th, but in the body of Christ, there is no such concept. We are all dependent upon each other and wholly dependent on God. We are God's vineyard, family, flock, and Christ's body, made up of many members.

Please remember that my brother -- hey bro, what's that measurement again?

GO. AHEAD!

PAY MY VOWS

Offer God a sacrifice of thanksgiving and pay your vows to the Most High; Call upon Me on the day of trouble; I will rescue you and you will honor Me. -Psalm 50:14-15 (NASB)

The psalmist encourages the reader to make an offer, a sacrifice of thanksgiving to the Lord.

What an appropriate exhortation for the troubled times we live in now: the COVID-19 pandemic, racial tensions, political unrest, unstable governments, and financial uncertainty.

And yet, each of us is called to give the Lord an offer of thanksgiving—to "thank" Him for the good he has provided and the kindness he has shown in recent months. The Most High God is worthy of our praise and thanksgiving because of His attributes and character; our human condition is not an excuse to withhold His praise; in fact, our condition helps us to call on Him with urgency; and at the beginning of every prayer, request, and petition, there should be an element of thanksgiving.

And after we have thanked God, **we pay our vows**, the promises we probably made at the beginning of this year—we give Him what we vowed in our hearts. He already gave us his best: salvation through Jesus Christ.

GO. AHEAD!

PRIDE: THE KRYPTONITE OF MAN

You younger men, likewise, be subject to your elders; and all of you, clothe yourselves with humility toward one another, because GOD IS OPPOSED TO THE PROUD, BUT HE GIVES GRACE TO THE HUMBLE. **-1 Peter 5:5 NASB**

In comic books, kryptonite is the green substance that renders Superman powerless. I've been in the church all my life and I've seen it happen repeatedly: the spirit of pride destroying a man.

Pride is arrogance, self-exaltation, and an overestimation of one's own worth. It is a terrible mindset (sin) and will ultimately destroy us if we allow it.

Men struggle with pride... we really do. It is the thing that prevents us from crying out to God, confessing our sins to another man, apologizing to our wives, and loving them as we are commanded.

Brothers, don't lose your "kingdoms" because of pride. Submit to God, resist the devil and he will flee. As men of God, let's humble ourselves before Him... right now!

"Father, we confess our prideful ways to You. May we see the example of your Son, Christ Jesus, who humbled himself to die for us. Humble us through your Word and the power of your Holy Spirit. Amen."

Walk in humility...

GO. AHEAD!

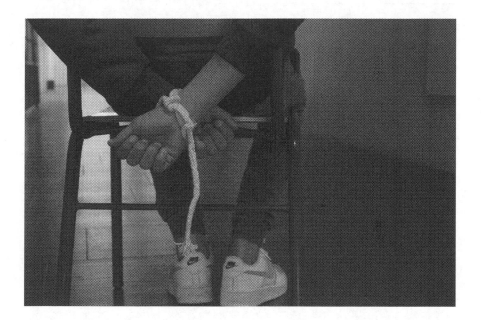

SERVANTS, NOT SLAVES

One of our ministers said on Sunday that we are servants, not slaves. That is a profound statement and is true. For the rest of our lives, we must consider who we are, WHOSE we are, and decide on how we will act, live, and conduct ourselves.

"That he no longer should live the rest of his time in the flesh to the lusts of men, but to the will of God." -1 Peter 4:2 KJV

The scripture tells us our lives should be to do God's will and not our own selfish pleasures. Death will result in the former; life will be reflected in the latter.

Brothers, we are servants of the Most High God! Let's remind each other of that.

GO. AHEAD!

STANDING IN THE FACE
OF OPPOSITION

Then in a furious rage Nebuchadnezzar gave orders to bring in Shadrach, Meshach, and Abednego. So these men were brought before the king. **- Daniel 3:13 CSB**

"But even if he does not rescue us, we want you as king to know that we will not serve your gods or worship the gold statue you set up." **- Daniel 3:18 CSB**

In all my preaching and pastoral ministry, I've taught from Daniel 1-3 more times than any other passage in the Bible.

The courage and bravery of four young men, who were taken from their homeland, stripped of their identity, and forced to live in a conflicting culture, is amazing to me and should be inspirational to all of us. These were young men, with much to live for back in Jerusalem, being the brightest and most cunning of their generation—only for their future to be drastically changed because of the disobedience of the nation (Judah).

I can't but help to think about today's youth, many of them bright, gifted, and talented-yet their lives are being drastically changed as well (COVID, school shootings, toxic social media influence) by the disobedience in our nation (America).

Nebuchadnezzar, the most powerful man on earth at one time, decides to erect an image of gold in his likeness. A command is issued that whenever the sound of music is played, everyone is to fall down and worship the golden image that the king set up; whoever refuses will be cast into a fiery furnace.

Word is brought to the king that these 3 Hebrew men (Daniel's presence is not recorded) refused to bow to his image-Nebuchadnezzar has them summoned to his throne chambers where they are asked again in front of everybody whether they will bow.

Shadrach, Meshach, and Abednego say something that requires great faith and courage in God: **"We will not serve your gods, nor worship the golden image you set up!"**

Nebuchadnezzar is furious at their conviction. His face changes and he orders them thrown into the fire, which is heated 7x hotter.

There are people all over the world who are standing in the face of opposition and refusing to bow to pressure: Born-again believers and Christians in Afghanistan, Nigeria, Ethiopia, Saudi Arabia, China, and Russia, to name a few. They are standing, not bowing.

Are you hypnotized by the "music" of this culture or are you listening to GOD? We in America have little time left before we're required to really stand for Jesus Christ. Little time is left before people's faces change toward us because we choose to stand for God in a world bowing to image after image after image…

I'm so encouraged by these young Hebrew men. Every time we read these passages; we should be reminded that standing for God is always better than bowing to the enemy/culture of this world.

Stand brothers.

GO. AHEAD!

STRONGER THAN YOU THINK

The temptations in your life are no different from what others experience. And God is faithful.

He will not allow the temptation to be more than you can stand. When you are tempted, he will show you a way out so that you can endure. -1 Corinthians 10:13, NLT

Temptations can range from seemingly harmless distractions to life-threatening addictions and everything in between. Where does yours fit in? The irony is that this one thing that's so personal to you is a struggle for many others too. Remember, that in many ways, you are not alone. Trust in God and lean on Him for the strength to overcome them each day. Only He (Christ) has the power to make you stronger than you think.

But he said to me, "My grace is enough for you, for my power is made perfect in weakness." -2 Corinthians 12:9a NET

I don't know about you, but that's encouraging news!

GO. AHEAD!

THE GOOD SOLDIER

Reading: 2 Timothy 2:3-6 ESV

3. Share in suffering as a good soldier of Christ Jesus. 4. No soldier gets entangled in civilian pursuits, since his aim is to please the one who enlisted him. 5. An athlete is not crowned unless he competes according to the rules. 6. It is the hard-working farmer who ought to have the first share of the crops.

Here are some examples of what our lives should look like:

1. a good soldier
2. an athlete who competes according to the rules
3. a farmer who works hard to partake of his crops

I'd like to share more on #1: being a good soldier of Jesus Christ. If you ever served in the military, you'll remember that after you enlisted and completed your military entrance processing station (MEPS) training, you were sworn in.

Everyone who joins the military has one thing in common: they must swear in by repeating the military oath of enlistment or military oath of office. From the oath, it is made clear that you will be defending the Constitution—not a person. Discipline and accepting orders are sworn to.

But everyone who is born again into the Kingdom of God has one person in common: His name is Christ Jesus, and we make allegiance to

Him as our commanding officer. In the natural, we "joined" the military... in salvation, Christ chose us to be soldiers!

Brethren, will you please the one who has called you to be a soldier? Or do you insist on doing things your way—ignoring and disregarding the commandments of our Lord?

When a person is called to the military and assigned to battle, they cannot be consumed with the cares of life or back home; it will be a detriment to the mission. As sons of God called into spiritual battle, we cannot be consumed with the things of this world. If so, it will be a detriment to our souls. The greatest liberty we'll ever have is by serving the Lord Jesus Christ, the Commander of the Lord's Army.

GO. AHEAD!

Be a good soldier!

THE ATHLETE

An athlete is not crowned unless he competes according to the rules. -2 Timothy 2:5 ESV

Last time, we talked about the good soldier... Let's talk about the athlete today.

Athletes train and sacrifice their bodies. That is the cost they pay to be the best, to excel in their given sport. Then there is the mental training and internal resilience that must be achieved to reach a higher level of competition.

And then, tragically, when the time comes for one to compete, they can find themselves disqualified. What?!

- The runner who moved before the gun was fired...
- The swimmer who dived into the pool before the signal...
- The receiver who catches the ball, but his foot is out of bounds...
- The weightlifter or bodybuilder who used steroids...

All of the training, proper diet and bodily exercise will not matter at all if you and I do not compete according to the rules. The "rules" for us men in our daily lives are the commandments of God. According to 1 John 5:3, His commandments are not grievous, which means weighty or burdensome. God's rules and laws make our way better, and brighter, and bring safety and protection. They are a "joy" to keep and a "burden" to disobey.

Men, live your lives according to the Word of God.

You'll be crowned someday!

GO. AHEAD!

THE HARD-WORKING FARMER

It is the hard-working farmer who ought to have the first share of the crops. Think over what I say, for the Lord will give you understanding in everything. **-2 Timothy 2:6-7 ESV**

To review and recap, this is what our lives should look like:

1. a good soldier
2. an athlete who competes according to the rules
3. a farmer who works hard to partake of his crops

Brethren, are we pleasing the one who has called us? Are we living our lives according to the "rules" or laws of God? And finally, are we working hard to be the "first partaker of our crops?" How does this question even apply to our lives in the year 2022?

Farming is hard work! And it carries a great responsibility. You can't be lazy or unconcerned if you're going to be a farmer. It will require getting up early and working late so the fruit of your labor can be a blessing to so many others you don't even know. Imagine a farmer working all day, week, month, and year and **never** being able to enjoy what he has grown or cared for.

Living for Jesus is not easy! Being a disciple of Christ carries a great responsibility. Work hard and endure the difficult conditions so you can receive a "harvest" of wisdom, knowledge and understanding.

David Guzik said this in his commentary on 2 Timothy 2:

- The soldier who stops fighting before the battle is finished will never see victory.
- The athlete who stops running before the race is over will never win the race.
- The farmer who stops working before the harvest is complete will never see the fruit of his crops.

Brothers, consider what the Lord wants us to understand in 2022. Perseverance is how the goal is reached.

GO. AHEAD!

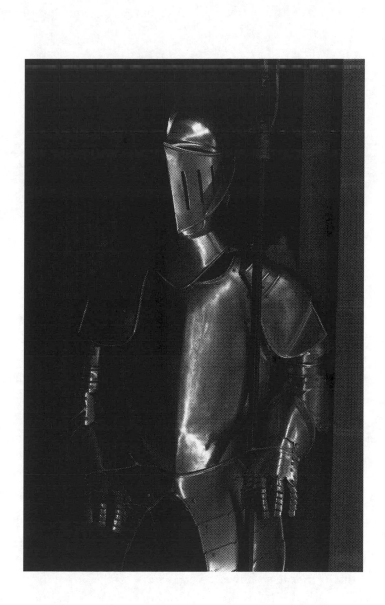

THE WHOLE ARMOR

Imagine this: before leaving your house this morning, you must decide which article of clothing to remove. Will you leave without your shirt? Maybe your pants?

(That's kind of funny). What about your shoes? No belt?

I know this seems like a silly example, but it's meant to be. You see, almost every day we take a chance and leave the house unprepared for what the day's events will bring. "Put on the whole armor, that ye may be able to stand against the wiles of the devil," Ephesians 6:11 KJV says. In a hurry, we leave the house not properly clothed and protected against the schemes of the enemy. I am guilty of this some days, my brothers. When I have on the WHOLE armor of God, I am ready and engaged. But when I forget to pray or I am not truthful (the belt), there is a feeling of anxiety instead of confidence (in God).

Brothers, we just can't afford to walk in this fallen world without the full armor of God. There are too many casualties on the battlefield: from pastors to deacons to worship leaders to business owners to maintenance workers to barbers... the devil (our enemy) has no respect for what we do—only for WHO we are and HOW we live our lives in the power of Christ—that is legitimate power!

Verse 13 goes on to encourage us to take on the full armor of God so we can withstand the evil day. That time is now, sons of God. Are you dressed and ready? When I was in boot camp for the Naval Reserves, we would look each other over before a major inspection. Soldiers point out things to each other that can go overlooked or minimized. These deficiencies are corrected, so when the commander or someone of great importance does a major inspection, a passing grade is given.

GO. AHEAD, and make sure you have ALL your armor on. It's a fight out there. You need to be ready, my brother.

UNDER AUTHORITY

Luke 7:2 CSB
A centurion's servant, who was highly valued by him, was sick and about to die.

Luke 7:6 CSB
Jesus went with them, and when he was not far from the house, the centurion sent friends to tell him, "Lord, don't trouble yourself, since I am not worthy to have you come under my roof.

Luke 7:8 CSB
For I too am a man placed under authority, having soldiers under my command. I say to this one, 'Go,' and he goes; and to another, 'Come,' and he comes; and to my servant, 'Do this,' and he does it.

The words spoken by this Roman centurion in verse 8 are some of the most powerful recorded in Scripture; he says something that every man/brother needs to recognize… "I too am a man placed under authority."

May I translate? *I have someone over me who tells me what to do. Yep.*

You just know I'm going to ask this: whose authority are you under? Who or what directs how you live your life, spend your money, and spend your time? Someone is over us, and we absolutely need to know who or what that governing authority is.

When I worked at PB Atlantic, I knew I had a Vice President of IT who had our back, upheld our mission, was vested totally in our development, and was concerned about our physical and mental well-being. So, when we worked and were met with resistance from difficult people, we would mention his name in conversation. We were under his authority, and he submitted himself to his authority.

As Dr. Tony Evans said, "the key to great faith is to be operating under legitimate spiritual authority"!

There is a name and person that carries great authority, and you and I need to place our very lives under him, Jesus Christ.

<u>The centurion sent a message to Jesus:</u>

"That is why I didn't even consider myself worthy to come to you. **But say the word, and my servant will be healed.**"

Now, that is great faith… because Jesus is the ultimate power and authority!

GO. AHEAD!

WAITING... AND
NOT ASHAMED

"Indeed, let no one who waits on You be ashamed; let those be ashamed who deal treacherously without cause." -Psalm 25:3 NKJV

I don't know if it's ever happened to all of you, but for those who did, remember waiting for your mom or dad to pick you up after school? After football or band practice or some other after-school activity, there you are waiting for your ride to come...

One by one, all your classmates and friends start leaving, and there you are standing there—still waiting, and feeling a little embarrassed. I can remember this so many times. But no matter how long you must wait, eventually, your ride pulls up and you are relieved. You're just happy to be going home.

Waiting on God is a patient activity. One must trust and believe God is going to show up (He always does... just ask the Hebrew boys. Or ask Habakkuk, the prophet).

Don't let what you and I think is a delay make you ashamed. Our God will never disappoint. Those who deliberately sin, reject Christ, and deny God, let them be ashamed.

Not you, my brother. You love Him... with all your heart, soul, mind, and strength. Hold that head up!

GO. AHEAD and keep trusting GOD!

WE ACT LIKE WE DON'T KNOW

Even an ox knows its owner, and a donkey recognizes its master's care—but Israel doesn't know its master. My people don't recognize my care for them. Isaiah 1:3 (ESV)

We had this cat for a while. When I got up, he would just look at me, and occasionally rub my leg and keep going. But when my wife woke up, he would "meow" and follow her all over the house, not letting her out of his sight. Do you know why? She was the one who fed him. I would like to believe I am the joy of my granddaughter's life. I know she loves "Papa" and I love her dearly. Yet when she hears my wife coming downstairs, she jumps out of my lap and follows my wife right into the kitchen. She does this because she knows breakfast is coming soon.

An animal and a little child know something that we as a people seem to have no clue about: they know who takes care of them.

- Our nation is in real trouble. And God's people seem to have an identity crisis:

The nation has rejected God, and we the Lord's people act as if we don't belong to Him; we act like we don't even know Him!

This was the Prophet Isaiah's dilemma back in his day: he was instructed to prophesy to a people (children) who had rebelled against God (Father), who always nourished them well and provided for them.

… but we act like we don't know this. This country and its citizens continue to push and edge God out of every domain, business, enterprise, industry, and organization, but what concerns me is God's people not understanding they are God's people.

Know ye that the LORD he is God: it is he that hath made us, and not we ourselves; **we are his people,** *and the sheep of his pasture.* (Psalms 100:3 KJV, emphasis mine)

The Scripture uses two dumb animals to indict us for our rebellion and ignorance of who our true "owner" and "master" are. The ox, in all his brute strength, submits its will to the owner and serves him. The donkey recognizes where its provisions are kept and, even if turned loose, will find its way to them.

Why can't we strive to be even like the lowly ox and donkey and say this morning, "Father God, You are the one who nourishes me; You are my owner and master—I recognize Your care for me."

GO. AHEAD!

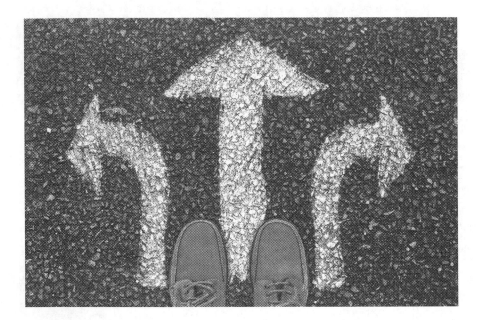

WHICH DIRECTION

Do you ever wonder where you should be going in life... or what "truth is... or how you can make your life better?

Welcome to the mindset of billions of other people on this earth. Everyone is looking for these things through the "things" around them. This is called a worldview. People shape their idea of direction, truth, or happiness from a collection of attitudes, values, stories, and expectations about the world around them, which inform their every thought and action. (https://rb.gy/dtthas)

Let me summarize: People use the world's values to determine how they eventually think and act!

Thomas asked the question: "Lord, we don't know where you're going... how can we know the way?" Thomas is literally asking Jesus "which way should I be going?"

Every man on this devotional thread has asked this same question at one time in his life.

The "way" really isn't a path or highway, but a person: Jesus said unto him, *"I am the way, the truth, and the life. No one can come to the Father, except through me."* (John 14:6)

Brother, how do you know you're going the right way with Jesus Christ in your life? How can you be sure? Are you seriously relying on TV networks and social media sites to know the truth and find your way?

Jesus says, "I am THE way!" The Greek language suggests the only proper path; the road that's been traveled and proven.

GO. AHEAD!

Jesus will lead you to the Father.

WILLING TO BE HELPED

And if one prevail against him, two shall withstand him; and a threefold cord is not quickly broken. -**Ecclesiastes 4:12 KJV**

Good morning, brothers. Read verse 8 after you read verse 12. You'll see a man who is successful, ambitious, and productive, but he is alone. There is no one to share his rewards or success with. Then the preacher of Ecclesiastes raises an important question: why is he working so hard and for whom will it benefit?

In warfare, whether spiritual or physical, relationships are important, and yes, critical. If I am opposed by something or someone, I have a friend or brother (Prov.17:17 KJV) who can help me withstand and overpower him.

So, brethren, where is your brother-in-arms to help you fight the enemies that rage against your soul and mind? Who is your brother in adversity? Who is your friend and accountability partner?

We ALL need someone to help us at certain times; don't be fooled by this coronavirus pandemic and think isolation means separation. We have the privilege of text, conversation, and prayer to stay in touch with each other so we can stay committed to God. It is a burdensome task to "walk" alone with no help.

GO. AHEAD… ask for HELP.

WORDS AND MEDITATION

Let the words of my mouth, and the meditation of my heart, be acceptable in thy sight, O Lord, my strength, and my redeemer. (**Psalm 19:14 KJV**)

The reservoir, the container of man—**his heart.**

Over the course of our lives, we've placed a lot of things in our hearts.

Some are good and noble. Others are very questionable. There are even things that are shameful and kept secret.

And yet, the human heart can contain both bad and good; noble and vulgar; courage and fear; aspiration and defeat; love and hatred.

But what does the heart of a man look like who has surrendered to the Lord?

The first thing you will notice is **his words**. His use of words, their tone, effects, and their impact on others.

The psalmist first prays for the words he speaks. In the Bible, James 3 gives us powerful insight into how much harm is done with our tongue and concludes by saying no man can tame it. Brothers, I've come to realize only the Holy Spirit can help us speak the right words.

And then the psalmist prays for his **heart meditation**: what does he think about, what captures his thoughts throughout the day, and what is he planning next? Will it be good and honorable, or will it be displeasing to the Lord? So, with great humility, the psalmist prays for his external words and internal meditation and acknowledges the Lord Jesus Christ as his strength and kinsman-redeemer: He will/can help us to say and think the right things.

The human heart is deceitful and desperately wicked. Who can know it? Our God does.

So, let's pray,

Father God,

I humbly ask You now to speak to the hearts of every man who holds this devotional in their hands. Let them know You are their Creator and desire for each one to be in the right relationship with You. The Scriptures declare this was made possible through Your Son, Jesus Christ, who satisfied every requirement so we could have eternal life and be saved from the penalty of sin and death.

Through the Spirit of adoption, make men "sons" and transform us from slaves to sin to servants of righteousness.

For this, we say, "thank You" and we glorify You as the only wise God, our Savior.

We pray this humbly in the name of Jesus.

Amen!

Printed in the United States
by Baker & Taylor Publisher Services